SELECT Recipes

Easy, Healthy And Tasty

With the option of cooking without meat

AIDA REGALADO VÁSQUEZ

First of all, I want to thank You for buying this recipe book.

*M*y goal is for my children, and all those who care for their health and that of their loved ones, to have this recipe book handy, which I have compiled throughout my 48 years living in California. I hope that you enjoy some of these favorite recipes from Mexico, the Mediterranean and Asia.

As the title of the book says, there are three reasons why you should have this recipe book. The recipes are EASY to prepare. They have few ingredients and preparing them is so simple that anyone can have these dishes ready in little time, even if you are a novice in the kitchen! I always focused on those of us who work and have very little time to cook.

My second goal is for the food to be HEALTHY. As you can probably tell, most of the ingredients consist of fresh fruits and vegetables, with the option of adding some kind of meat if you so desire. To me, health comes first, and I was very mindful of ingredients that are considered to be Superfoods, such as asparagus, bell peppers, broccoli, celery, roma tomatoes, zucchini, avocado, cilantro, chili, lemon and beans, among others; and of course, all seasonal fruits. In each of the recipes you will even find a little information about the benefits of some of the ingredients.

And the third reason why I chose these recipes is that the dishes are TASTY! While eating healthy, we won't have to give up those dishes that we grew up with in California. Nothing beats freshly-cooked homemade enchiladas, guacamole prepared using only fresh ingredients, or delicious salmon tacos which, in addition to being super-nutritious, can be prepared in just a few minutes. How about homemade hummus to share?

And most of all, the ingredient that can't be missing from any of these recipes is a dash of Love. Which means that this recipe book was written with lots of love for you and your loved ones. Aida Vásquez

Aida Regalado Vásquez

Recommendations

As I already mentioned, these recipes were selected first and foremost with a focus on health, in order to stay well nourished and have a long life filled with energy and free from painful illnesses that are also a burden to our families.

I recommend that once a week you sit down with your partner and children and plan your weekly menu, where you will pick 6 or 7 breakfasts, lunches and dinners to your liking. In this recipe book I also included a few recipes to prepare flavored fruit water and some teas recommended for common ailments.

Once you decide on the dishes to be prepared, you only need to make a shopping list for 3 days. I don't recommend buying all the groceries you'll need for the week because it is better to have fresh vegetables and seasonal fruits, which are not only cheaper but also more nutritious and delicious.

It is also preferable to check your fridge and pantry to check whether you already have some of the ingredients. What you can indeed buy in advance for the entire week are legumes, spices, oils and tortillas. Remember to prepare the vegetable broth for the week (recipe included).

And lastly, to prepare the meals faster during the week, it is preferable that you wash, dry and chop the vegetables so they are ready when the time comes to prepare the food. It is much easier and faster to have the cilantro already chopped; the onions and bell peppers already julienned or diced and the cheese already crumbled, than to take everything out of the fridge and prepare it when tired or hungry after getting home.

And, of course, there must always be a fresh homemade sauce in your fridge, either for snacks, to add to your tacos or quesadillas, or to offer to your visits with tortilla chips.

Table of Contents

Before you start cooking

- Read the recipe to know how it is prepared.

- Prepare all the ingredients and measure and weigh each. only leave on the counter what you need, so you can clean up as you cook.

- Have cups and spoons handy to measure the ingredients. I also recommend buying a good scale!

- As soon as you are done using each ingredient store it back in its proper place and clean as you go. remember if you already have all the ingredients on the counter, you won't forget to add them.

Saffron Rice

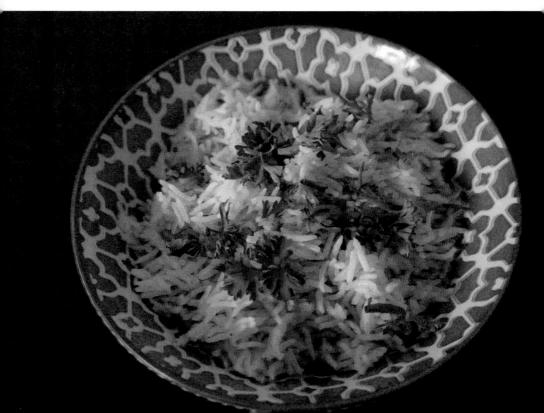

Ingredients:

1 ¼ cups of Basmati rice
¼ chopped small onion
1 tablespoon of olive oil
30 saffron threads or more, to taste
2 cups of vegetable broth
¼ cup of finely chopped parsley
Salt & pepper to taste

Preparation:

- First, rinse the rice about three times and let it drain.

- Heat the oil and fry the chopped onion until it is transparent.

- Mix the saffron with the vegetable broth and let it soak for a few minutes.

- Add the rice to the pan with salt and pepper. Add saffron and broth mix. Slow cook for about 20 minutes. Add more broth if necessary.

- Once the rice is cooked, serve it, and you can sprinkle it with grated cheese or some finely-chopped parsley.

Side Dish:

Saffron is loaded with Vitamin C which is a great antioxidant. Also Saffron helps relieve stomach aches, cramps, gases, constipation, abdominal inflammation, insomnia and muscle pains.

Rice With Spinach

Ingredients:

1 cup of brown rice
2 tablespoons of finely diced onion
3 tablespoons of minced parsley
3 cups of water
4 cups of chopped spinach
1 teaspoon of garlic
4 tablespoons of oil
Salt & pepper to taste

Preparation:

- Sauté the rice in the oil

- Add the garlic and onion and fry for a minute

- Add the spinach and water; when it starts to dry, add the salt and parsley. Slow cook for approximately 15-20 minutes.

Side Dish:

Spinach and chard contain provitamin A and, especially, a good amount of folic acid, which is quite important for the skin and hair; as well as proteins, iron, vitamins and minerals

Mexican Rice

Ingredients:

1 ½ cups of rice
3 Roma tomato
½ small onion
2 cloves of garlic
1 cup of vegetable mix (carrots, green beans, corn)
2 cups of vegetable broth
Boiling oil
Salt to taste

Preparation:

- Rinse the rice thoroughly about three times and drain.

- Heat the oil and stir-fry the garlic until it browns, ensuring to stir constantly to prevent it from getting charred.

- Remove the garlic and blend with the Roma tomatoes, the onion and the vegetable consommé.

- Add the sauce to the rice and, as soon as it boils, add the vegetables and more salt if necessary. Lower the flame, cover with a lid and let it cook for 14 to 15 minutes.

Side Dish:

Roma and regular tomatoes are rich in vitamins and minerals: this vegetable contains vitamin C – a powerful natural antioxidant – in addition to vitamin A, K, iron and potassium. Helps eliminate toxins.

Oatmeal & Apple

Ingredients:

1/2 Apple per person
1/2 Cup of oats per person
1 Tablespoon of honey per serving
1 Tablespoon of cinnamon powder

Preparation:

- Cook the oats and cinnamon in water or almond milk.

- When served on the plate, add the sliced apple and cover with honey to taste.

- Can be accompanied by a whole wheat bread toast.

Benefits Of Oats:

It is a very energizing food, and great for your brain, as well as a semi-laxative! The soluble fiber in oats is good for people suffering from diabetes.

Steamed broccoli with soy
and ginger sauce

Ingredients:

1 cup of broccoli per person
1 teaspoon of low sodium soy sauce
1 teaspoon of grated ginger
1 teaspoon of lemon juice
1 teaspoon of water
Pepper if you like (does not need salt)

Preparation:

- Steam cook the broccoli until it is soft, yet crunchy – 4 minutes more or less.

- Drain and transfer to a bowl, where you will add the soy sauce, ginger, lemon juice and water.

Side Dish:

Broccoli – Prevents breast, uterus and prostate cancer, as well as cancer in internal organs such as liver, colon, kidney and intestine. Has a high content of vitamin A, C and E, amino-acids, zinc and potassium.

Broccoli With Chile De Arbol
And Spaghetti

Ingredients:

12 Ounces of spaghetti
1 Lb. of broccoli sliced into small squares
1 -2 Finely chopped chiles de arbol
½ Finely chopped red bell pepper
3 Tablespoons of olive oil
salt & pepper to taste

Preparation:

- In a large pot, boil water and salt. Cook the spaghetti for about 10 minutes until al dente. Drain.

- In another pot, boil salted water and boil the broccoli for 2 minutes.

- Meanwhile, heat the oil and stir-fry the chile de árbol and red bell pepper over a slow flame for about 5 minutes.

- Add the chiles, bell pepper, broccoli and oil onto the pasta and broccoli. Mix well and add salt & pepper to taste. Serve right away.

Broccoli:

Strengthens the bones, prevents breast cancer. Healthy during pregnancy. Offers intestinal vitality and reduces the impact of glucose.

Zucchini With Cheese & Cilantro

Ingredients:

2 Zucchinis
1 Tablespoon of unsalted butter
¼ Cup of finely diced fresh cilantro
¼ Cup of fresh cheese
Salt & pepper to taste

Preparation:

- Slice the zucchini into approximately ½ inch slices.

- Heat up the butter and sauté the zucchini; flip and sprinkle with a little salt.

- Sprinkle with cilantro. Brown for a little while and serve on a serving dish.

- Sprinkle with fresh cheese and serve.

Side Dish:

Zucchini contains high levels of potassium, vitamin B, dietary fiber and antioxidants, all of which offer great health benefits. It may even help regulate blood sugar levels, which can be quite beneficial for diabetics.

Sinaloa style deviled shrimp

Ingredients:

½ tablespoon of butter, softened
2 tablespoons of olive oil
1 tablespoon of chopped garlic
2 tablespoons of chopped pearl onion
Juice from 2 lemons
Salt & pepper to taste
1 kilogram of large headless shrimp
3/4 cup of ketchup
1 tablespoon of Maggi® Juice
1 can (105 grams) of adobo-marinated chipotles (Add Chipoltes to your taste. two or three chiles might be enough)

Preparation:

- Mix half of the butter, olive oil, garlic, onion, lemon juice, salt and pepper in a bowl. Add shrimp and stir so that they are thoroughly covered.

- Heat the remaining butter in a pot over a slow fire. Pour the shrimp and marinade mix, and cook until they get rosy, from 3 to 5 minutes.

- Blend the ketchup with Maggi® Juice, the chipotle and salt until you get a homogeneous sauce. Pour it on the shrimp and cook while stirring, until the sauce starts to boil. Lower the flame to a slow fire and cook for a few more minutes until the sauce has thickened.

- Serve with white rice and slices of avocado.

Dinner:

Shrimp is an excellent source of lean protein. Each 6 Oz. serving contains 39 grams of protein - a significant portion of the 46 gram daily intake recommended for women and 56 grams for men.

Green Chilaquiles

Ingredients:

16 dry tortillas
4 cloves of garlic
½ onion
3 or 4 Serrano peppers
1 ½ pound of tomatillos
1 cup of vegetable broth
Frying oil
1 cup of sour cream
½ cup of fresh cheese
Shredded chicken, if you like

Preparation:

- Start by browning the corn tortillas, previously cut into small triangles.

- Boil the chili and two cloves of garlic in a large pot with plenty of water for 5 minutes. Add the washed tomatillos to the pot and boil for another 5 minutes. As soon as their color changes, strain everything and let it cool before blending.

- Blend the tomatillos, chili and two more cloves of garlic, add the cilantro, onion and salt, and blend for a little while longer.

- Heat the oil in a pan and in low heat fry the sauce for 10 minutes, covering the pan with a lid. If it is too thick, add more broth.

- Before serving, heat the sauce and add the tortillas that you will serve. Serve and cover with extra sauce, cheese, cream and shredded chicken, if you like.

Breakfast:

Tomatillos are a good source of dietary fiber, niacin, potassium and manganese, iron, magnesium and more. They help prevent bloating and tumors that may lead to cancer growth.

Chow Mein

Ingredients:

1 pack of noodles or egg noodles
½ cup of green beans
2 tablespoons of sesame oil
2 carrots sliced into sticks
4 small onions
½ broccoli separated into equally-sized pieces
A small pack of baby corn
½ red bell pepper cut into strips
4 tablespoons of soy sauce
1 tablespoon of grated ginger
1 cup of chopped cabbage
1 cup of vegetable broth
Steak, chicken or tofu if you like

Preparation:

- First prepare the noodles as per the instructions on the package.

- In a large casserole or wok, heat the sesame oil and sauté the vegetables, starting with the broccoli, then the green beans, carrots, onions, baby corn, red bell pepper and cabbage.

- Separately, mix the vegetable broth and soy sauce with and grated ginger.

- Add the vegetables, mix well and add the cooked noodles. Serve right away.

Dinner:

Sesame oil contains vitamin E, in addition to lecithin, which improve memory and protect nerve cells. All of these substances are essential for a healthy brain and to prevent a number of diseases, including Alzheimer's.

Crepes

Ingredients:

4 eggs
$\frac{1}{4}$ teaspoon of salt
2 cups of flour
2 $\frac{1}{4}$ cups of milk
$\frac{1}{4}$ cup of melted butter
Preparation:

Preparation:

- In a bowl, mix well the eggs with the salt.

- Slowly add the flour and milk - a cup of flour and a cup of milk…

- Add the butter and whip until the mix is smooth.

- Put in the fridge for at least one hour before preparing the crepes.

- Fill with marmalade, jam, strawberries, bananas, blackberries, mango, and garnish with whipped cream and powdered sugar to taste.

Breakfast:

Having fruit for breakfast in the morning is recommended for all ages, from children to the elderly. And accompanying the crepes with seasonal fruit is the best breakfast for everyone in your family.

Red Enchiladas

Ingredients:

6 Guajillo dried chiles [use California chiles if you don't like spicy food]
3 Pasilla dried chiles
3 Roma tomato
¼ onion
2 cloves of garlic
1 ½ cups of vegetable broth
18 corn tortillas
1 cup of fresh shredded cheese
½ cup of sour cream
½ teaspoon of marjoram
Salt to taste

Preparación:

• Clean, de-seed and devein the chilis, then roast them. Soak in a container with hot water for 20 minutes.

• Meanwhile, roast the Roma tomatoes and peel them. Also roast the onion and garlic.

• Transfer the chili to a blender along with the Roma tomatoes, garlic, marjoram and vegetable broth, and blend well.

• Heat a little oil in a pot and fry the sauce for ten minutes. Add salt to taste.

• Dip the tortilla in the sauce (you can also dip the tortillas with the sauce and fry with a little oil) and transfer to a large plate, fill with refried beans, cheese, potatoes or shredded chicken.

• Roll up and cover with more hot sauce.

• Garnish with sliced onion or minced lettuce, crumbled cheese and a little sour cream.

Dinner:

Corn tortilla is not only super-tasty, but it also packs a lot of energy since it is high in carbohydrates. It is rich in calcium, fiber and potassium. And not only is it nutritious and low-fat, but also cheap!

Nopalitos Salad

Ingredients:

1 Dozen tender nopales
1 Small onion
¼ Cup of finely chopped cilantro
2 Medium-sized roma tomatoes
1 Garlic
1 Lemon (for juice)
1 finely chopped jalapeno chili

Preparation:

- Boil the already-chopped nopales in plenty of water with ½ onion, garlic and salt (for about 5 minutes).

- Once cooked, put them in a colander to drain dry.

- Put them in a salad bowl and mix with the cilantro, the other half of the onion and chopped Roma tomatoes.

- Add salt to taste and the lemon juice. You can also add finely chopped jalapeño chili if you like.

Side Dish:

Nopal is a hypoglycemic agent; in other words, it reduces blood sugar concentrations. It is also a great source of soluble and insoluble fiber which helps lower cholesterol and triglycerides.

Greek Salad

Ingredients:

2 tablespoons of red wine vinegar
1 tablespoon of finely chopped fresh parsley
1 tablespoon of olive oil
1/8 teaspoon of salt
1 large Roma tomato diced into medium-sized dices, or cherry tomatoes
1 chopped, seedless cucumber
1/4 finely sliced red onion
2 tablespoons of Greek or feta cheese

Preparation:

- Combine vinegar, oil, parsley and salt in a large bowl.

- Add the Roma tomatoes, cucumber and the onion.

- Mix well and sprinkle with cheese when serving.

Lunch:

Onions have few calories – only 45 apiece. They are low in sodium and have no fat or cholesterol. They contain fiber, which is essential for a good digestion and to provide a feeling of fullness. And they also improve your mood!

Mediterranean Salad

Ingredients:

12 cherry tomatoes
2 Persian cucumbers
¼ red onion
¼ green bell pepper
¼ red bell pepper
¼ yellow bell pepper
½ cup of black olives
A little oregano
¼ cup of feta cheese
Salt, olive oil and vinegar to taste

Preparation:

- Wash and chop all the vegetables. Dice the bell peppers and cucumbers. Cut the olives and tomatoes in half, and julienne the onion.

- Also dice the cheese.

- Mix all of the ingredients together and, before serving, add the salt, oil, vinegar, cheese and sprinkle with a little oregano.

Side Dish:

Bell peppers have essential antioxidants, which are fundamental for your body. The also contain very important fibers to deal with constipation issues. This is in addition to minerals such as potassium, magnesium, phosphorous and calcium.

Entomatadas With Sour Cream

Ingredients:

8 Roma tomato
1\2 onion
2 jalapeño chili
5 oz. of fresh cheese
A few leaves of romaine lettuce
12 tortillas
2 cloves of garlic
4 oz. of sour cream
1 teaspoon of cumin
1 sliced red onion

Preparation:

- Cook the chili peppers with the garlic and tomatoes. Blend with the onion, cumin and salt. Transfer the sauce to a pot and keep warm.

- Fry the tortillas for a little while and dip in the sauce; fill with whatever you like. Put them in a leaf of lettuce and add a little more sauce. Garnish with onion slices and a little sour cream and cheese.

Lunch:

Tomatoes are high in fiber, and contain water and low in calories. They have vitamin A, C and E, which are considered to be antioxidant and beneficial to the immune system, while their potassium keeps the body hydrated and prevents pains or cramping.

Spaghettis And Zucchinis With Chipotle Sauce

Ingredients:

1 pack of spaghetti

2 zucchini spireled like spaghetti

2 cloves of garlic, chopped

1 stick of butter

1 cup of heavy cream or half-and-half

2-3 adobo-marinated chipotle chili, or more if you like your food spicy

1 can of mushrooms or a cup of fresh mushrooms preferably

Salt & pepper to taste

3 tablespoons of Cotija cheese

Preparation:

- Fill a large pot with water and add a little salt. Let it boil on a high flame and add the spaghetti. Cook uncovered, occasionally stirring until the pasta has completely cooked but still feels firm (about 10 minutes).

- Meanwhile, melt half the butter in a large skillet over a medium flame. Stir-fry a clove of garlic until it looks transparent, as well as the zucchini spaghetti and the mushrooms for one or two minutes. Set it aside. Blend the cream, garlic, chipotle chili, salt and pepper. Cook on the large skillet for a couple of minutes, always stirring.

- Once the pasta is ready, drain it and mix it with the rest of the butter until it melts. Transfer the pasta, the zucchini and mushrooms to the skillet with the chipotle sauce, mix well. Add more salt and pepper to taste. Serve and sprinkle with the Cotija cheese.

Dinner:

Chipotle chili strengthens the immune system. And the healing properties of the chipotle chili can lower the cholesterol and triglycerides in the blood.

Baked Asparagus With Sesame And Onion

Ingredients:

1 pound of asparagus
2 tablespoons of sesame oil or olive oil
¼ tablespoon of roasted sesame
2 tablespoons of small onions, sliced
Salt and pepper to taste. Sea salt recommended.

Preparation:

- Preheat the oven to 450°

- Cut off the hard stem of the asparagus, wash and dry with a paper towel.

- Put the asparagus in a 9 X 13 inch baking pan

- Mix the oil with salt, pepper, onions and thoroughly cover the asparagus with this.

- Bake the asparagus from 12 to 14 minutes until they brown and get softer.

- Roast the sesame and sprinkle on top of the asparagus.

- Asparagus contain very few calories and are high in fiber. Their high amount of antioxidants help us fight free radicals, which cause illnesses and aging.

Side Dish:

Asparaguses contain very few calories and are hugh in fiber. Their high amount of antioxidants help us combat free radicals, which cause illnesses and aging

Fajitas

Ingredients:

¼ pound of bacon, diced (optional) or 2 tbsp olive oil
2 medium-sized onions, julienned
2 cloves of garlic, finely chopped
1 red bell pepper, de-seeded, julienned
1 green bell pepper, de-seeded, julienned
1 yellow bell pepper, de-seeded, julienned
1 pound of tenderloin tips (optional)
2 tablespoons of soy sauce
2 tablespoons of seasoning sauce (e.g., Maggi®)
1 pack of corn tortillas
1 sliced avocado
Minced cilantro and sauce to taste
Salt & pepper, to taste

Preparation:

- Put the bacon or olive oil, onion, garlic and peppers on a skillet over a medium flame and stir-fry until the peppers are soft.

- Add the meat and cook, (this is optional) stirring from time to time, until it has lost its red color. Add the sauces: soy sauce, seasoning Maggi sauce, pepper and, if necessary, a little bit of salt.

- Heat the tortillas and, when serving, you can accompany the fajitas with avocado, cilantro and a sauce of your choice.

Dinner:

The tortilla is an essential food, since it provides 50% of carbs, 39% of proteins and 49% of our daily calcium intake requirements.

Guacamole

Ingredientes:

2 ripe avocados
¼ onion, finely chopped
1 jalapeño or Serrano chili if you like your food spicy
½ bunch of cilantro, finely chopped
2 lemons (for juicing)
½ Roma tomatoes, finely diced

Preparación:

- Cut avocados in half and remove all of the pulp using a spoon.

- If you have a mortar & pestle, grind the avocado; otherwise you can use a fork to mix well.

- Add the onion, chili, cilantro and Roma tomatoes and mix well.

- Lastly, add the salt and lemon juice. Make sure everything is thoroughly mixed.

If you won't serve it right away, put the seeds of the avocados into guacamole and store in a sealed container. Put away in the fridge – it's tastier when served cold.

Side Dish:

Avocado contains natural fiber, which prevents constipation, keeps a healthy digestive system and reduces the risk of colon cancer.

Hummus

Ingredients:

1 cup or can of cooked chickpeas
½ cup of Tahini
2 cloves of garlic
Juice from 2 lemons
2 tablespoons of olive oil
½ teaspoon of paprika
Salt & pepper to taste

Preparación:

- In a food processor or blender, grind the chickpeas along with the Tahini, garlic, olive oil, lemon juice and water. Add salt & pepper to taste. If the mix is too thick, you can add a little more olive oil.

- Serve on a large dish, garnish with olive oil and sprinkle paprika on top. Can be decorated with a few olives.

Snack:

Chickpeas have a high fiber content, which helps stave off constipation, reduces the possibility of suffering from intestinal illnesses and calms hunger. They are always part of vegan diets.

Baked Apples Stuffed With Raisins Or Blueberries

Ingredients:

1. Apples, one per person
2. Tablespoons of raisins or blueberries per apple
3. Bee honey, agave nectar or maple syrup
4. Cinnamon powder

Preparation:

Carefully core the apple and stuff it with raisins or blueberries. pour the honey, nectar or syrup on top and sprinkle with the cinnamon. Bake for 1-2 minutes in the microwave or oven until they get soft.

Dessert:

Apples contain a soluble fiber called pectin, which helps reduce blood cholesterol and prevents it from pooling on the walls of the blood vessels.

Molletes With Beans & Cheese

Ingredients:

4 bolillos o teleras (short baguette) cut in half
$1/2$ pound of manchego cheese
1 cup of refried beans
1 cup of pico de gallo.   See recipe

Preparation:

- Spread refried beans on the bolillos halves.

- Add slices of manchego cheese to cover the beans

- Put in the oven for a few minutes until it is au gratin

- Cover with the pico de gallo sauce and serve.

Lunch:

Black beans are an excellent source of energy due to their high protein content and low fat. Black beans are also high in magnesium and contain a high amount of potassium and iron

Vegetable-Filled Egg Omelet

Ingredients:

3-4 eggs
1 tablespoon of sun-dried Roma tomatoes
3 tablespoons of chopped red and green bell peppers
2 tablespoons of water
1 tablespoon of butter
1 tablespoon of any cheese of your liking
Salt & pepper

Preparation:

- Omelet preparation:

- Whip the eggs well, adding salt and pepper. Don't let it go foamy.

- In an 8-inch nonstick skillet, melt the butter and spread it all over the skillet.

- Add the whipped egg and move the skillet side to side so that the egg spreads into a thin layer.

- Cook and fill half of the omelet with the filling of your preference. Roll it up like a taco and decorate with a little cheese. Serve with your preferred sauce.

Omelet filling:

Stir-fry a tablespoon of sun-dried Roma tomatoes and chopped red and green bell peppers. Season with salt & pepper. When filling the omelet, you can also add a little cheese.

Breakfast:

Egg *benefits: a single egg contains 6 grams of protein, which satiates and ensures that we don't overeat. Egg also contains antioxidants, which can even improve your eyes' health.*

Avocado Toast

Ingredients:

4 slices of toast
1 avocado
1 lemon
1 tablespoon of olive oil
6 cherry tomatoes
Salt & pepper to taste

Preparation:

- Cut the avocado into small pieces.

- Add salt and pepper and crush it. Add lemon juice and mix well with salt and pepper.

- Toast the bread. If you prefer, spread some butter on it.

- Cover the bread with the avocado mix and spread it well.

- Decorate with the tomatoes and a few cilantro leaves.

- Sprinkle with a few drops of olive oil and serve.

Breakfast:

Avocado contains two chemical compounds that act as eye antioxidants and can decrease damage and reduce the risk of developing age-related macular degeneration.

Homemade Potatoes With Onion
And Bell Pepper

Ingredients:

1 ½ pounds of potatoes, peeled and diced into ½ inch dices
½ cup of red onion, diced into ¼ inch dices
1 red bell pepper, cut into ¼ inch squares
3 tablespoons of olive oil
2 tablespoons of butter
Salt & pepper to taste

Preparation:

- Boil the potatoes in a pot with plenty of salted water. As soon as the water starts boiling, let them cook for a minute, remove them and drain on a colander.

- Heat the oil in a frying pan and stir-fry the bell pepper a little; add the potatoes and stir-fry for 10 minutes until they brown.

- Add the onion and butter and keep cooking until the potatoes are soft. Add salt and pepper to taste.

- Serve hot.

Breakfast:

Potatoes contain plenty of magnesium, potassium and other minerals. Magnesium is particularly good to strengthen the immune system.

Papaya with Yogurt

Ingredients:

1 Cup papaya per person
½ Cup of natural greek yogurt per person
2-4 Dates per person
1 Whole-wheat bread toast per person

Preparation:

- Slice or dice the papaya to your liking and serve on a white dish with the yogurt.

- In a separate dish serve the dates, or you can chop them and mix them with the yogurt if you prefer to sweeten the yogurt.

- Accompany with the toast.

Breakfast:

Papaya is very good for dealing with indigestion since it is semi-laxative. It also helps relieve throat and ear ailments. **Dates Are Amazing!** They contain vitamins, minerals, carbohydrates, sugars and fiber. Dates also have a laxative effect, improve cardiovascular health and help with tiredness.

Pasta With Zucchini And Mint

Ingredients:

1 pound of linguine
2 pounds of finely sliced zucchinis
A small bunch of chopped pepper-mint
5 teaspoons of olive oil
1 tablespoon of finely chopped garlic
Salt and pepper to taste

Preparation:

- Preparation

- Cook the pasta in a pot with boiling water and salt as per the instructions on the package.

- Meanwhile, fry the slices of zucchini in a pan along with the garlic until they soften.

- Drain the pasta and mix it with the zucchinis, the mint, salt and pepper to taste.

- Add the rest of the oil and serve right away.

Dinner:

Zucchini - It is a major source of potassium, which helps control arterial pressure by reducing the sodium in the blood, which makes it ideal for people with hypertension.

Quinoa With Vegetables

Ingredients:

1/2 cup of quinoa
1 cup of water or vegetable broth
3 teaspoons of soy sauce
2 cloves of garlic, finely chopped
2 cups of chopped vegetables, such as carrots, broccoli, celery, zucchini, bell peppers.
1 tablespoon of olive oil
Ground pepper to taste

Preparation:

- Wash the quinoa and boil it along with a cup of water or broth. As soon as the water starts boiling, add one clove of garlic, cover with the lid and let it cook for 15 minutes.

- To prepare the vegetables: heat the oil in a frying pan and fry the other clove of garlic with the vegetables. Add just a little pepper.

- Add the quinoa to the mix and add the soy sauce. You do not need salt since if your soy sauce is already salted.

- Cook for a few minutes and serve.

Lunch:

Quinoa is high in proteins when compared to most vegetables, and contains all the essential amino-acids that the human body needs.

Salmon With Vegetables

Ingredients:

1 pound of wild caught salmon
½ pound of broccoli
1 small onion
1 bunch of asparagus
3 carrots
½ cup of lemon juice
Salt and pepper to taste

Preparation:

- Preheat the oven to 350 degrees.

- Place the pieces of salmon on aluminum foil. Add the lemon juice, a little salt and pepper, and let it marinate for half an hour.

- Cut the vegetables and season with salt and pepper to taste.

- Cover the salmon with the vegetables and chopped onion and wrap thoroughly with another piece of aluminum foil.

- Bake in the pre-heated oven for 30 minutes.

Dinner:

Salmon is a blue, fatty fish that contains about 11 grams of fat for every 100 pounds of meat -- a content that is on par with sardines or tuna. The fat is rich in Omega-3, which helps reduce cholesterol and triglyceride levels.

Roma Tomato Sauce

Ingredients:

4 Roma tomatoes
1/2 Onion
2 Cloves of garlic
1 Fresh jalapeño pepper
1/2 tablespoon of marjoram
¼ teaspoon of ground cumin
A pinch of dry oregano
Salt to taste

Preparation:

- In a pot with water, boil the jalapeño chili along with the garlic cloves for 2 minutes. Add the tomatoes and boil for another 5 minutes.

- Peel the tomatoes and transfer them along with the jalapeno and garlic to the blender. Add the onion, marjoram, cumin and salt to taste.

Side Dish:

Serve in a bowl and sprinkle with oregano. This sauce is super tasty to accompany tacos dorados or an egg in the morning.

Pico De Gallo

Ingredients:

2 Roma tomatoes, diced
1 small onion finely
2 finely chopped Serrano or jalapeno
(less spicy) peppers
1 or 2 lemons for juicing, to taste
½ cup of finely chopped cilantro
Salt to taste

Preparation:

- Mix the tomatoes, onion and chili peppers in a bowl and stir well.

- Add the salt, lemon juice and cilantro and mix well. Cover it and put it in the fridge to serve it cold.

Side Dish:

Lemon is known mainly due to its high vitamin C content, B-complex vitamins, calcium, iron, magnesium, potassium and fiber.

Stir Fry Vegetables

Ingredients:

2 1/2 tablespoons of olive oil
2 carrots cut into sticks
1/2 cup of green beans
2 zucchinis cut into sticks
1 tablespoon of soy sauce
1/2 tablespoon of sesame oil
1 1/2 tablespoons of sesame seeds
Chicken or steak, diced (Optional)

Preparation:

- Heat up 1/2 tablespoon of olive oil and brown the sesame seeds for just a minute. Set them apart.

- Cook the green beans for two minutes in salted water.

- Heat up the rest of the olive oil and stir-fry the carrots and zucchini for two minutes. Add the green beans and fry for another minute.

- Stir-fry the vegetables for 2-3 minutes and add the soy sauce and sesame oil. Mix well and serve, sprinkle with sesame seeds when serving. If you like you can add shredded chicken or pieces of steak.

Dinner:

Green beans contain plenty of fiber, which helps lower high cholesterol. They also help prevent obesity.

Red Lentil Soup With Vegetables

Ingredients:

2 tablespoons of olive oil
1 small onion, chopped
1 rib of celery, chopped
1 chopped carrot
2 cloves of garlic, finely chopped
1 minced Roma tomatoes
4 cups of vegetable broth
½ cup of red lentils
2 tablespoons of dry parsley
1 ½ tablespoons of SUMAC – the ingredient that gives it a delicious flavor.
1 lemon
Salt & pepper to taste

Preparation:

- Heat up the oil in a pot. Add the onion, celery and carrot for 3 minutes. Add the garlic, tomatoes and vegetable broth.

- Cover with the lid and slow cook for 20 minutes. Let it cool down and blend. If you want, you can strain the soup.

- Add the lentils to the soup and keep cooking for about 12-14 minutes, until the lentils are soft. Add the parsley and SUMAC. Season and add the lemon juice.

Lunch:

Celery: Helps with digestion, combats gases and abdominal bloating. In addition, it helps normalize menstruation and relieve the symptoms of menopause.

Tacos Ahogados

Ingredients:

1 pound of tomatillo
2 to 3 Serrano chili peppers, to taste
2 cloves of garlic
1 small onion
1 small bunch of cilantro
½ pound of fresh cheese
1 dozen tortillas
1 tablespoon of oil to fry sauce and more if you prefer to fry the tortillas
Salt & pepper to taste
Optional for filling :shredded chicken; mashed or boiled potatoes, or cheese.

Preparation:

- Boil the chili peppers in a pot with plenty of water for two minutes.

- In the same pot with boiling water, add the peeled, washed tomatillos. As soon as their color changes, take everything out of the boiling water.

- Blend the chili peppers, garlic, ½ onion and ½ bunch of cilantro with salt. Fry the sauce in a little oil for 5 minutes.

- Heat or fry the tortillas and fill the taquitos with chicken, potatoes or cheese. Wrap.

- Mix the ½ onion, fresh cheese and ½ finely chopped cilantro in another container.

- Serve the taquitos, cover with the warm sauce and sprinkle with a mixture of cheese, onion and cilantro..

Lunch:

Tomatillo contains a high amount of antioxidants, as well as vitamin C, phosphorous, calcium, salts, minerals and iron. In addition to their anti-carcinogenic properties, tomatillos are a great source of fiber.

Crunchy Potato Tacos

Ingredients:

12 tortillas
3 large potatoes
1/2 cup of fresh cheese
1/2 chopped lettuce
frying oil
salt & pepper to taste
Roma tomato sauce (see included recipe)
½ cup grated queso fresco, sour cream to taste

Preparation:

- Wash and peel the potatoes into one inch cubes and cook them for 15 to 20 minutes in a large pot with salted water until they feel quite soft when pierced with a fork.

- Drain the water and add cheese, salt and pepper to taste to the potatoes. Mash them well.

- Heat the tortillas to soften them and fill them with the potato mix.

- Heat up the oil in a large pan and brown the tacos. Remove the excess oil using paper towels.

- Serve the tacos with grated lettuce, cream, crumbled cheese and sauce.

Lunch:

Potatoes give you energy, and because they are high in fiber, they help with constipation and reduce bloating. They are good to be eaten by themselves, either boiled or raw (their juice). High in vitamins and minerals.

Cabbage & Radish Tacos

Ingredients:

1 cup of chopped red cabbage
$\frac{1}{2}$ cup of shredded chicken or meat if you prefer meat
6 or 8 thin sliced radishes
2 tablespoon of chopped cilantro
2 tablespoons of lemon juice
4 or 6 Corn or wheat tortillas
Salt & pepper to taste

* Chicken or meat are optional

Preparation:

Mix all ingredients well and serve as tacos or wrapped in wheat tortilla rolls.

Lunch:

Benefits of red cabbage

Helps improve eye health. Prevents issues such as constipation. Reduces cholesterol levels. Contains a large amount of vitamin C, which increases your defenses.

Salmon & Red Cabbage Tacos

Ingredients:

1 piece of salmon (see recipe for salmon with vegetables)
6 corn tortillas
1/2 red cabbage (grated)
1 tablespoon of chipotle chili juice or more, if you like your food spicy
Juice from one lemon
1 tablespoon of avocado mayonnaise
1 avocado
salt & pepper to taste

Preparation:

- Prepare the salmon and cut it into pieces.

- In a large bowl, mix the cabbage, the lemon juice and the chipotle, one tablespoon of mayonnaise, salt and pepper to taste.

- Heat the tortillas and fill them with a few pieces of salmon and plenty of cabbage in each taco. Accompany with a few slices of avocado.

Dinner:

Benefits of cabbage: Cabbage contains a high amount of calcium and is great for the skin. In addition, it is good for your kidneys, bladder and reduces obesity.

Bowl Of Greek Yogurt With Chia And Fruit

Breakfast was never as nutritious as this bowl full of fiber and energy to start your day. Balance your day with this bowl; the berries give it a unique and refreshing flavor.

Ingredients:

2 cups of Greek yogurt
¼ cup of agave nectar, honey, or maple syrup
¼ cup of blueberries
¼ cup of blackberries
¼ cup of chia (already soaked)
¼ cup of granola
1 sliced banana

It is best to add seasonal fruit, such as strawberries, mangos, kiwi, papaya or other types of fruit you like.

Preparation:

- In a blender, add the yogurt, agave nectar or honey, blackberries, blueberries and blend until everything is fully mixed.

- Serve the yoghurt in a bowl and garnish with the chia, granola, bananas, berries and fruit of your liking.

Breakfast:

Benefits of Chia: it has more Omega 3 than some fish, and Omega 3 helps reduce cholesterol and eliminate fat, while its large amounts of antioxidants combat aging.

Tortas Planchadas or Mexican Paninis

Ingredients:

6 bolillos or teleras (short baguettes)
One per person
6 tablespoons of fried beans
¼ grated lettuce
6 slices of red onion
12 slices of Roma tomato
1 red and 1 green bell pepper, juliened
6 slices of fresh cheese
6 Serrano chili peppers, either fresh or in vinegar
6 tablespoons of sour cream
1 sliced avocado

Preparation:

- Cut the bread in half, remove some of the stuffing and spread a tablespoon of beans on one half and 1 tablespoon of sour cream on the other half. Add one tablespoon of bell peppers. Heat for two minutes on a pan or Panini grill.

- Stuff with the Roma tomato, lettuce, fresh cheese, onions, chili peppers and avocado.

- If you like, you can add strips of grilled steak.

Lunch:

Avocado is full of vitamins and minerals — it provides these percentages of the reference daily intake: Vitamin K: 26%. Folic acid: 20%, Vitamin C: 17%, Potassium: 14%, Vitamin B5: 14%, Vitamin B6: 13%, Vitamin E: 10%! In addition, an avocado has more potassium than a banana.

Tzatziki - Yoghurt & Cucumber Sauce

Ingredients:

1 cup of flavorless Greek yoghurt
2 tablespoons of olive oil
1 peeled, finely diced cucumber
1 tablespoon of the juice from half a
lemon
1 ground clove of garlic
1 tablespoon of finely chopped spear-
mint
1/2 teaspoon of fresh, finely chopped
dill
salt & pepper to taste

Preparation:

In a large bowl, mix all of the ingredients and refrigerate for at least two to
three hours to let all the flavors combine. Served cold to garnish meats or
as an appetizer with triangles of pita
bread or vegetables.

Snack:

*This mediterranean appe-
tizer is very low-fat, refreshing,
and chock-full of high-quality
protein. in addition to being
easy to prepare, it's delicious!*

Waffles

Ingredients:

1 cup of Kodiak Cake Mix
1 cup of almond milk
1 egg
1/8 teaspoon of powdered cinnamon
2 tablespoons of ground flaxseed
2 tablespoons of butter

Preparation:

- Preheat your waffle iron while you prepare the mix.

- Mix all the ingredients well, except the butter, in a blender or mixer. If you don't have any of these appliances, you can use a fork or whisk beater.

- Let the mixture rest for about 5 minutes.

- Prepare the waffles, spreading a little butter on the waffle iron so that they don't stick.

- Serve them on a large plate accompanied with seasonal fruit, maple syrup, caramel syrup or whipped cream

Breakfast:

Just one tablespoon of flaxseed is loaded with great antioxidants such as omega-3, protein and fiber. Flaxseed might also help lower blood sugar and the risk of diabetes and heart disease.

Cucumber, Lemon And Chia Water

Ingredients:

1 cup of water
1/2 cucumber
2 lemons
2 teaspoons of Chia
4 cups of ice
6 leaves if mint
Sweetener to taste: Sugar, Agave, Honey, Stevia

Preparation:

- Wash the cucumbers thoroughly and blend well with a cup of water along with juice from the lemons and sweetener to taste.

- Strain and empty into the jar with ice, where you add the chia, a few slices of lemon, and a few mint leaves.

- Let it rest until the chia is well-soaked and serve!

Side Dish:

Benefits of drinking this water: Besides this water being super-delicious and refreshing, cucumber contains silica, which takes care of our skin and keeps us young. Having lemon with cucumber is also great for those who suffer from fatty liver disease. And chia is rich in fiber and antioxidants, which helps us prevent premature aging.

Hibiscus Water

Ingredients:

1 cup of hibiscus
5 cups of water
Sweetener to taste: Sugar, Agave, Stevia or Honey

Preparation:

- Rinse the hibiscus in cold water and put it in a pot of water. As soon as it starts boiling, turn off the flame.

- Let it cool down and strain into the jar that you will use to serve. Add the sweetener if you like and serve with plenty of ice!

Side Dish:

Benefits of hibiscus: Diuretic, helps with weight loss, helps eliminate toxins, reduces glucose levels (you don't consume sugar), helps reduce high blood pressure.... and besides being tasty, it is super-refreshing!!!!

Orange Water With Ginger And Mint

Ingredients:

5 cups of filtered water
3 oranges
½ tbsp. a little of fresh grated ginger
5 fresh mint leaves
Agave or Stevia to sweeten to taste

Preparation:

Blend the orange juice along with ginger and sweetener. Strain and mix with the cups of water and ice. Can be served with a few slices of orange and a mint leaf.

Side Dish:

Benefits of ginger: Improves digestion, prevents the flu and colds, alkalizes and helps reduce joint pain, among many others.

Spring Rolls

Ingredients:

1 pack of rice paper wrappers
1 bag of rice vermicelli
1 bag of Chinese roots
1 julienned red bell pepper
1 julienned yellow bell pepper
1 finely chopped pearl onion
4 tablespoons of basil and cilantro
1 julienned avocado
1 tablespoon of olive oil
Sriracha, Teriyaki or Chinese sauce,
best with Peanut sauce.
Salt & pepper to taste
You can add shredded chicken or sautéed shrimp if you like

Preparation:

- Prepare everything before you start wrapping. Put warm water in a large bowl to dip each rice paper.

- Soak the rice noodles in hot water until they change their color and get soft.

- In a skillet, sauté the Chinese roots, peppers and onion; season with salt and pepper.

- Moisten a few paper towels and use them to place the rice paper when wrapping, to prevent sticking.

- Soak a sheet of rice paper until it gets soft; do not over-soak so that it is easier to wrap.

- Fill with some of the noodles, vegetables, basil, cilantro and avocado. Wrap it tight as you would do with a burrito and you are done!

- Serve with any sauce

Lunch:

Chinese roots have a high content of vitamin A, B12 and C, high proteins, fiber and calcium. Furthermore, they contain nutrients that are easily digested, thereby preventing intestinal fermentation.

Strawberry Water With Lemon And Chia

Ingredients:

2 cups of water
5 lemons
1 pound or about 15 strawberries
2 teaspoons of chia (optional)
Sweetener to taste: Stevia, Sugar, Agave, Honey, or pure maple syrup.

Preparation:

- Wash the strawberries thoroughly and blend with a cup of water, juice from the lemons and the sweetener.

- Transfer everything to a jar and add the rest of the water, chia and a generous amount of ice. Decorate with slices of lemon and strawberries.

Side Dish:

A few benefits of strawberries: Eating strawberries improves your eye health, prevents colds, reduce blood pressure and help reduce cholesterol...

Not only that – it also keeps our skin and hair looking young!

Three-Lemon Water

Ingredients:

8 cups of water
2 yellow lemons
2 green lemons
2 Mexican limes
$\frac{1}{2}$ half of thinly sliced lemon to decorate
Sweetener to taste: Sugar, Agave, Stevia, Honey

Preparation:

- Wash thoroughly the two lemons and slice each into quarters. Juice the other four lemons

- Remove all the seeds, blend all the citruses for 3 to 4 pulses. Make sure they do not get ground, because the water will turn out too bitter.

- Strain and transfer to a jar with plenty of ice and the rest of the water, and sweeten to taste. Decorate with thin slices of the lemon.

Side Dish:

Benefits of lemons: Lemons are essential in our cuisine for many reasons. They help us alkalize our organism, help us eliminate toxins and are an antibacterial. And, of course, it is VERY refreshing.

My list of teas and
What they are good for

Green Tea	Antioxidant, Energy
Seven Blossoms Tea	Sleep, Relaxant
Chamomile Tea	Nausea, Sleep
Cinnamon Tea	Diarrhea, Flu
Basil Tea	Digestion, Flu
Spearmint Tea	Nausea, Digestion
Ginger Tea	Diarrhea, Cold
Rosemary Tea	Bloating, Gases
Lemon Tea	Flu and Colds
Orange Tea	Weight loss, Diuretic

The end

Select Recipes Easy, Healthy And Tastyl / Aida Regalado Vásquez

English Edition

Made in the USA
Middletown, DE
17 April 2022

63814650R00062